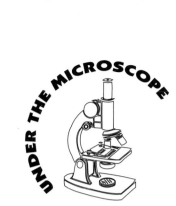

UNDER THE MICROSCOPE

OUR HOME

John Woodward

Gareth Stevens Publishing
MILWAUKEE

**For a free color catalog describing Gareth Stevens Publishing's list
of high-quality books and multimedia programs,**
call 1-800-542-2595 (USA) or 1-800-461-9120 (Canada).
Gareth Stevens Publishing's Fax: (414) 225-0377.
See our catalog, too, on the World Wide Web: http://gsinc.com

Library of Congress Cataloging-in-Publication Data

Woodward, John, 1954-
   Our home / by John Woodward.
     p. cm. – (Under the microscope)
   Includes index.
   Summary: Examines the tiny holes on a compact disc, the mites that live in
household dust, the coiled wire that brings light to our homes, and other
microscopic marvels.
   ISBN 0-8368-1602-1 (lib. bdg.)
   1. Science–Miscellanea–Juvenile literature. 2. Materials–Miscellanea–Juvenile
literature. 3. Engineering instruments–Miscellanea–Juvenile literature.
[1. Science–Miscellanea. 2. Microscopy.] I. Title. II. Series.
Q163.W646   1997
600–dc20   96-34486

First published in North America in 1997 by
Gareth Stevens Publishing
1555 North RiverCenter Drive, Suite 201
Milwaukee, WI 53212 USA

© 1997 Brown Packaging Partworks Ltd., 255-257 Liverpool Road,
London, England, N1 1LX. Text by John Woodward. All photos supplied
by the Science Photo Library, except pages 17, 21, 25: Tony Stone
Images. Additional end matter © 1997 Gareth Stevens, Inc.

Printed in the United States of America

1 2 3 4 5 6 7 8 9 01 00 99 98 97

CONTENTS

HARM AND HELP

Bacteria are found in almost everything. They are in food, the air, water, plants, and animals. They are tiny organisms that can be seen only with a microscope. Some bacteria are harmful, causing diseases (such as tuberculosis) and illnesses (such as food poisoning). But others are harmless and can even be helpful. For example, some kinds of bacteria are used to make yogurt, cheese, and other dairy products. Scientists utilize certain kinds of bacteria to make medicines.

The large purple object in this photograph is the head of a pin. The small, yellow objects are bacteria. The picture makes the point of just how tiny bacteria are.

BACTERIA-KILLING BACTERIA

• Some bacteria make a special substance that poisons other bacteria. Scientists use these killer bacteria to make medicines called antibiotics, such as penicillin. Antibiotics are used to treat diseases and illnesses caused by harmful bacteria.

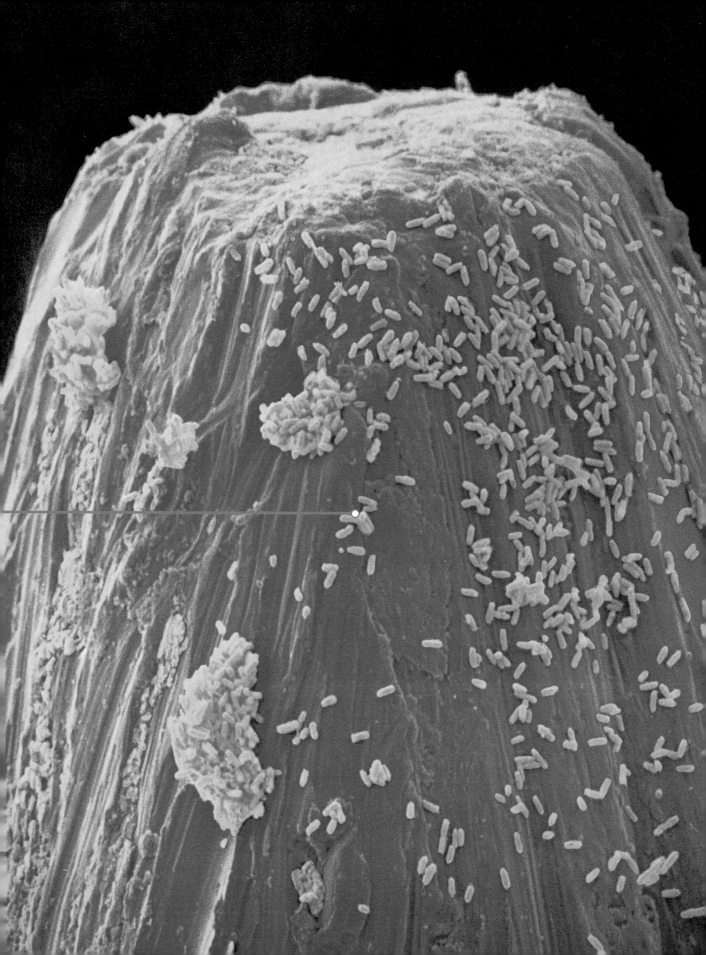

PLASTIC FOAM

Polyurethane is a human-made, or synthetic, substance that can be made into plastic foam. Some polyurethane foams are soft and easy to squeeze, like sponges. They are used to stuff cushions and pillows. Other types of polyurethane foams are more rigid. These are used, for example, as cores for airplane wings. One of the most unique features of polyurethane foam is that it keeps hot things hot and cold things cold.

Plastic foam is made when gas bubbles are added to polyurethane. The light areas are polyurethane, and the dark areas are gas bubbles.

LIMITED NATURAL RESOURCES

• Plastic is a synthetic material with many uses. A large number of household objects contain or are made of plastic. Most plastics are made from coal, petroleum, and natural gas. These resources are also used for fuel. Coal, petroleum, and natural gas are not renewable. That means when they are all used up, there will be no more on Earth.

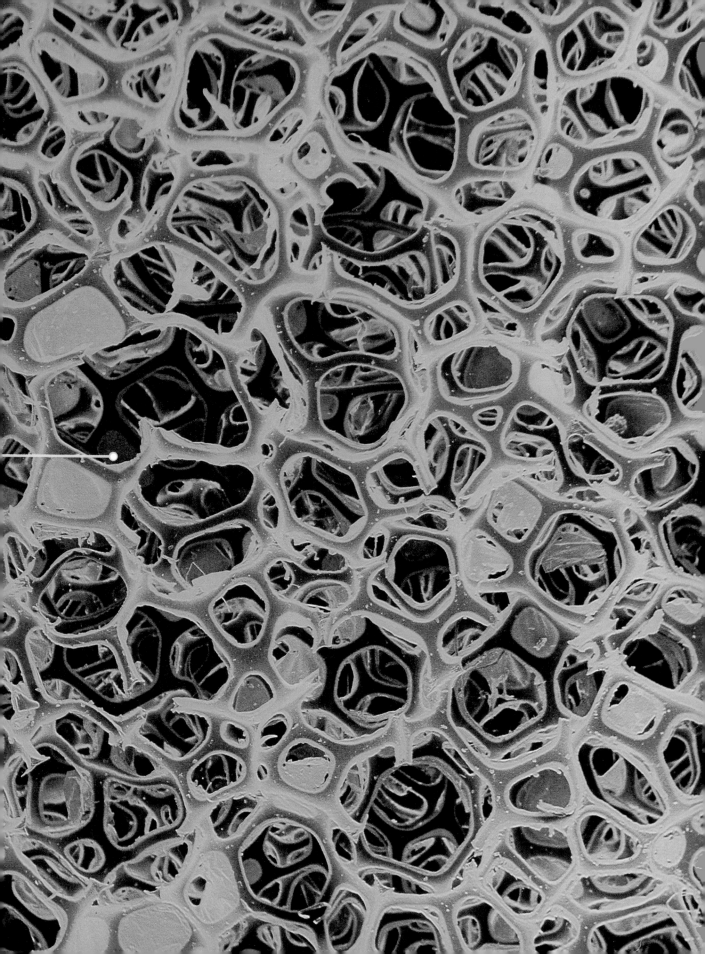

LIQUID PLASTIC

Polyester is a human-made, or synthetic, fiber. It is made from liquid plastic. The liquid is put into a container that is spun around at very high speed. As it spins, the liquid is forced out through tiny holes in a special machine called a spinneret. When the liquid comes through the spinneret, it hardens into a very long fiber known as a filament. The filament is then made into artificial yarns, such as polyester. Dacron is a polyester material. The holes in each yarn of Dacron trap air that keeps in heat. For this reason, Dacron is an excellent material for sleeping bags.

Pictured are polyester Dacron fibers used for insulation inside a sleeping bag. Each of the fibers contains up to seven air spaces. The spaces trap air.

GLASSY-EYED

- In the 1800s, an Englishman, Louis Schwabe, first made filaments from molten, or liquid, glass by forcing the liquid through tiny holes in a machine. When the liquid glass came into contact with cold air, it hardened into a fiber.

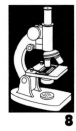

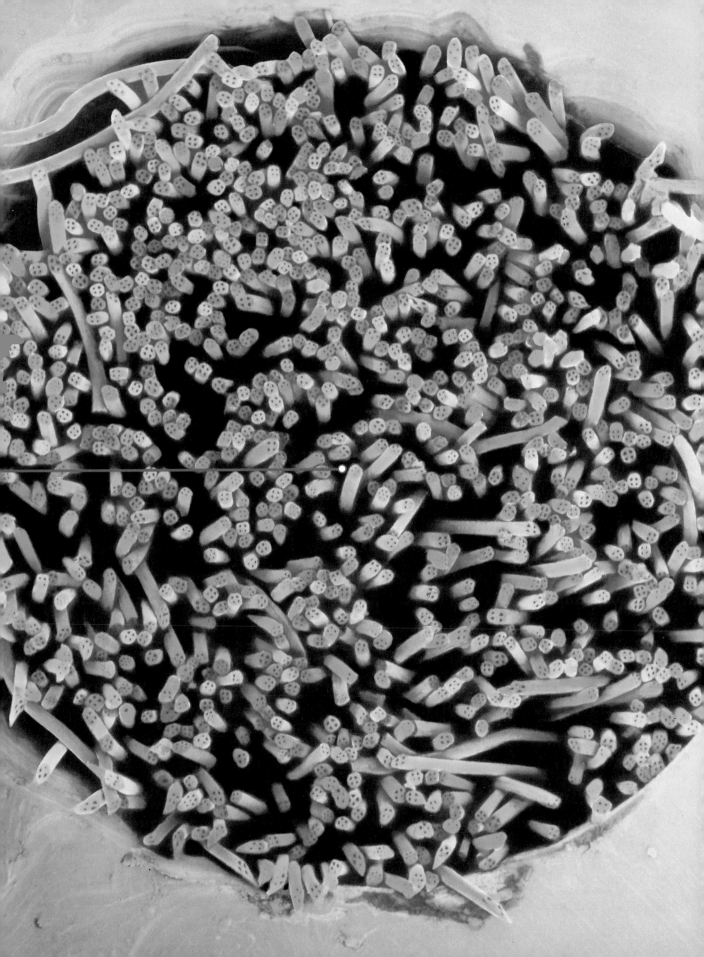

LIGHT INTO SOUND

The compact disc, or CD, that is used for recording sound was introduced in 1982. To make a so-called master disc, a laser beam is focused on a disc as it spins around at high speed. The laser beam is turned on and off, which cuts pits into the disc's surface. This master disc is then used to make copies onto other discs. When a compact disc is spun in a CD player, the pits either reflect or scatter light from a laser. The reflected light is changed into sound. Because there is no actual physical contact between the disc and the laser, the disc does not wear out.

This compact disc has actually been broken to reveal the pits that it contains. Each of the pits measures less than 1/100 of the thickness of a human hair.

INFORMATION EXPLOSION

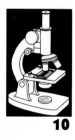

- At present, a compact disc can record almost 75 minutes of sound or video or over 100 million words. Researchers are now developing discs that can hold many times that amount of material.

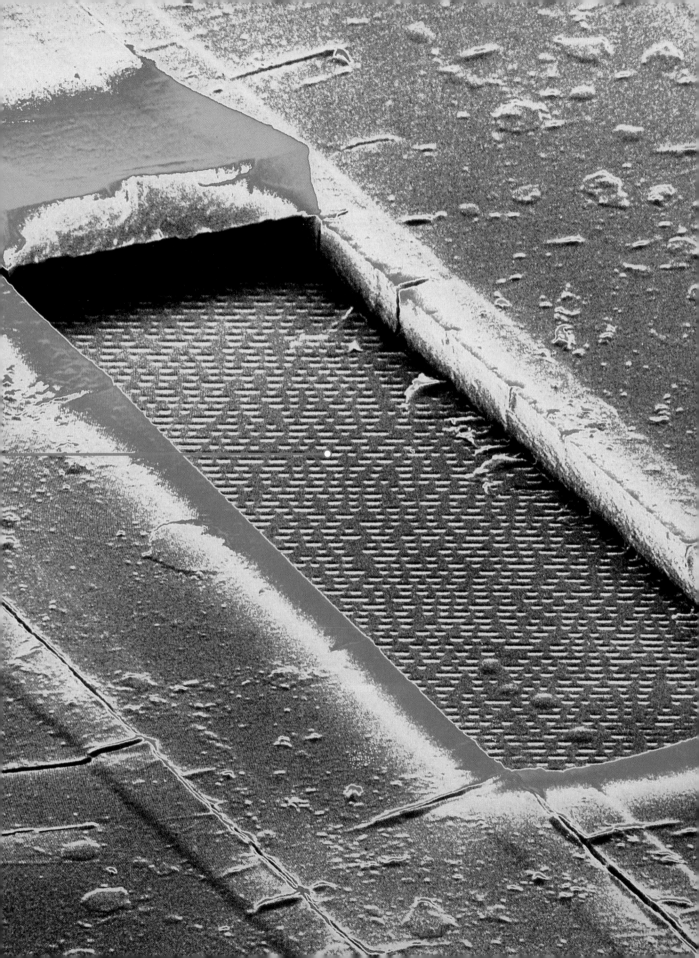

VELCRO PIONEER

A Swiss engineer named George de Mestral invented Velcro in 1948. De Mestral wanted to know why burrs from plants stuck to clothing and animal fur. When he looked at burrs under a microscope, he saw they were made of tiny hooks. These hooks fastened tightly around fibers of clothing and fur. De Mestral used his observations to make the material he called Velcro. Velcro serves a similar purpose to zippers and buttons. Among a multitude of other things, Velcro is used in space vehicles to attach objects such as food trays to surfaces to keep them from floating.

Velcro is made of two strips of material. One has tiny hooks. One has loops. When the two strips are pressed together, the hooks grip onto the loops.

MIGHTY VELCRO

- On a piece of Velcro .5 inch (1.3 centimeters) square, there are more than 700 hooks on one side and more than 12,000 loops on the other side.
- Velcro 2.5 inches (6.5 cm) square can support up to 1,000 pounds (454 kilograms).

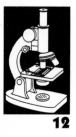

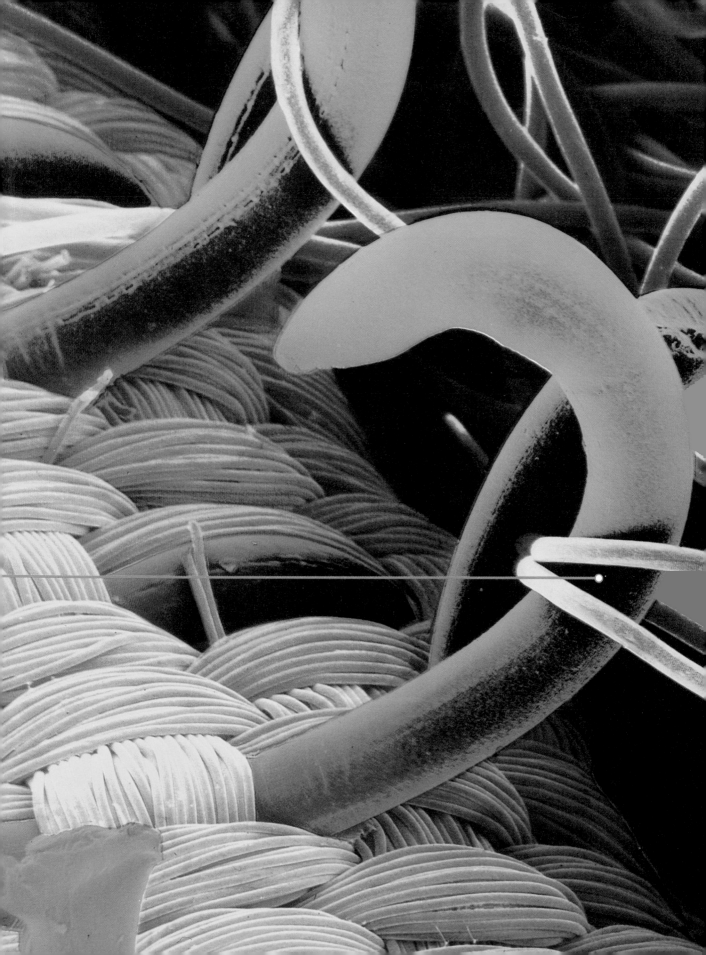

EASY WRITER

Felt-tip pens are markers that are fun to use, convenient, and clean. Inside the pen is a tube of thick ink. One end of the tube is joined to a nib, or tip, made of felt. The ink runs down the tube and flows through the nib. As the writer moves the pen across paper, ink flows onto the writing surface. The ink dries as soon as it reaches the paper. Felt-tip pens can be used for drawing as well as writing. Some felt-tip pens can even be used on surfaces such as plastic and glass.

Felt is made when wool or synthetic wool fibers are pressed together. That is why these fibers appear straight and not woven together like many other materials.

FIBER VS. FELT

• The nibs of pens with fiber tips are made from bundles of fibers held together with glue. Nibs of fiber-tips come in different thicknesses, from fine to thick. Fiber-tip pens last longer than felt-tip pens. They also do not lose their shape like felt-tips.

SMALL, BUT POWERFUL

Silicon is a nonmetallic element found in large quantities around the world. It is the main material of sand. Silicon is used in the manufacture of glass and electronic components that are known as transistors. Large numbers of transistor circuits can be etched directly onto one wafer of silicon crystal. These transistor circuits are the silicon chips that are so common in today's world. The chips are found in computers, space probes, wristwatches, calculators, washing machines, televisions, and much more.

Pictured is part of an integrated circuit on a silicon chip. The large globe is a connection point to other circuits. The connection is made along the gold wire.

DOWNSIZING

• In the past, computers were so big they completely filled a large room. Today, the various parts of a computer can fit onto a silicon chip that is no bigger than a fingernail.

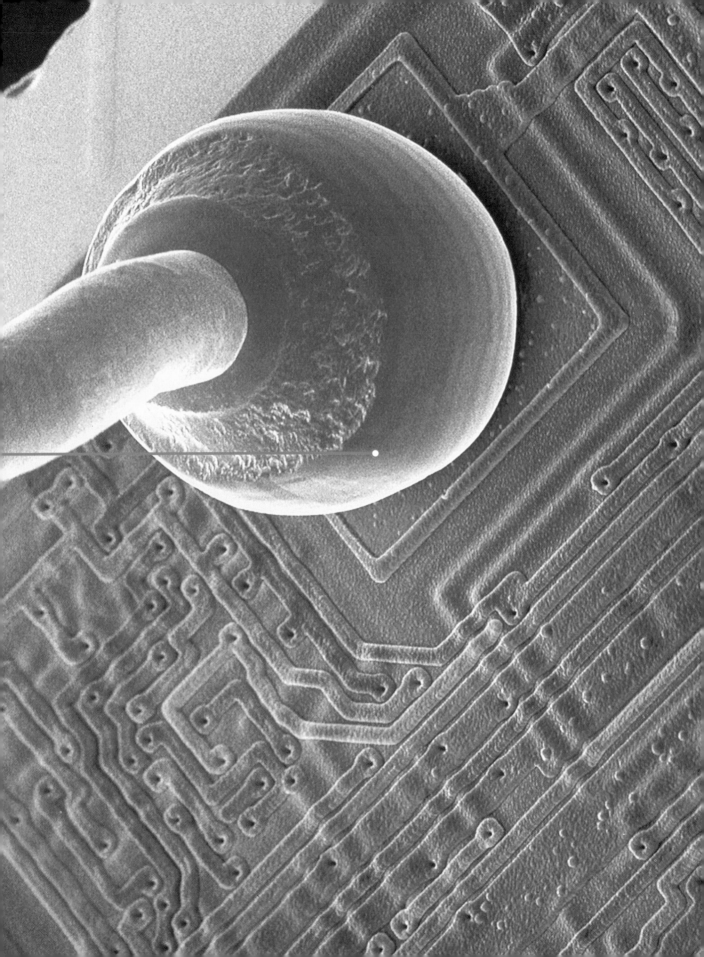

SEEING THE LIGHT

The part of a light bulb that gives off light is called the filament. It is a very thin wire, one-hundredth of a millimeter thick. The wire is usually made of a metal called tungsten. The filament is attached to thicker wires that run down a glass stem to the bottom of the bulb. When a switch is turned on, electricity passes through the filament and heats it. The filament becomes so hot that it gives off a bright white light. Light bulbs eventually burn out. The heat that makes the light also weakens the filament until it finally breaks.

The filament in a light bulb is made of a very long piece of wire. When it is wound into a tight double coil, the filament fits neatly inside the glass bulb.

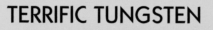

TERRIFIC TUNGSTEN

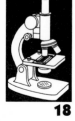

- Tungsten is a metal that can be heated to a very high temperature without melting. The tungsten filament in a light bulb reaches a temperature of 4,500° Fahrenheit (2,482° Centigrade). In comparison, water boils at just 212°F (100°C).

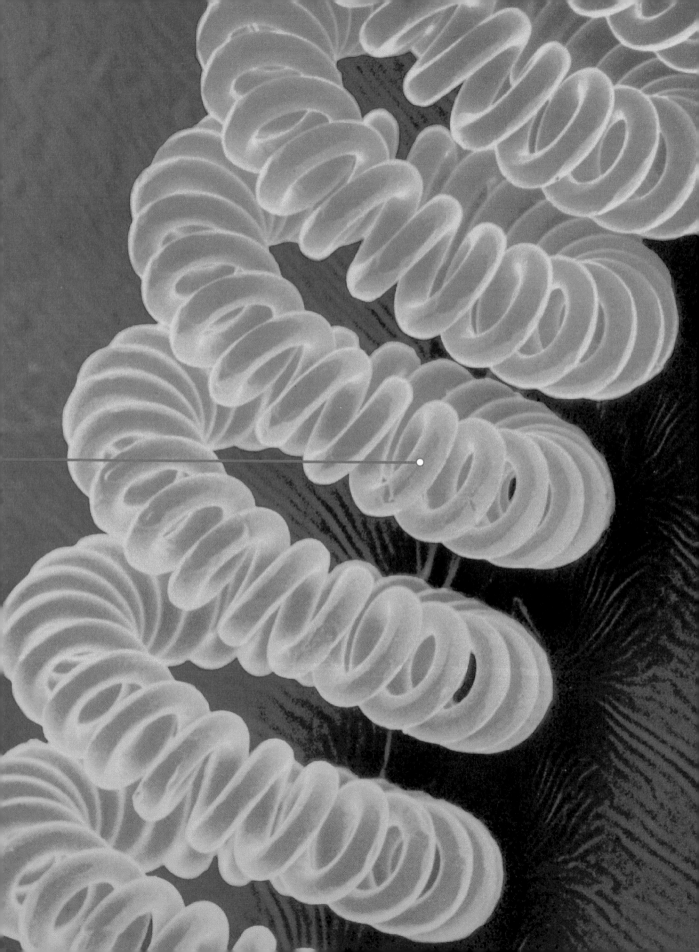

BITE THE DUST

Mites are very tiny animals that are related to ticks, spiders, and scorpions. These creatures may look like insects, but they belong to the group known as arachnids. Like all arachnids, mites have eight legs and rounded bodies. Dust mites are found everywhere that dust is found — in bedding, mattresses, pillows, curtains, carpets, and upholstery. They feed on the bits and pieces that make up dust, such as dandruff and other flakes of skin. Although dust mites do not directly harm humans, their droppings cause allergic reactions in many people.

The dust mite has four pairs of legs, two pairs of which are near the front of its head. Also on the front of the head are a pair of fangs and two shorter limbs similar to legs.

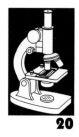

MITE SITES

• Mites live in all kinds of places, including some very odd ones. Some make their homes in the ears of moths, and others live on human skin. The cheese mite lives in decaying cheese.

DEVILISH DUST

House dust is a nuisance. This unwelcome visitor to our homes is a collection of many different plant and animal parts. Much of it is made up of the millions of dead cells that are shed from human skin every day. Human and pet hair, tiny insects, and plant material such as pollen also add to the dust collection. House dust can cause allergies in some people. Itchy skin and sore eyes are signs of this type of allergy. The allergy can also result in asthma.

The square object in the center of this photograph is a flake of human skin. The colorful strands surrounding it are fibers from clothing and furnishings.

A HAIRY SITUATION

- A single speck of dust contains an amazing number of objects. One large contributor to dust is human hair. An adult human has about 100,000 hairs on her or his head and loses between 20-100 hairs every day.

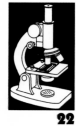

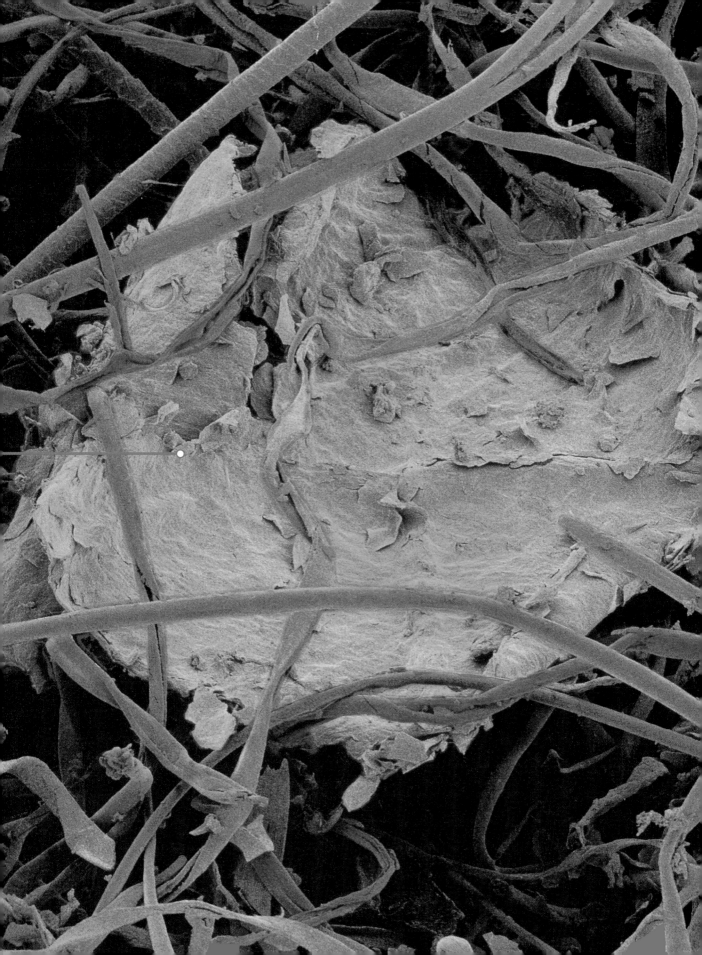

SPINNING YARNS

Cotton is a natural material that is used to make cloth. It comes from the cotton plant, which is a small flowering shrub. As the flowers die, they are replaced by round seed cases called bolls. When the bolls are ripe, they burst open into round, creamy white fluffy balls. This fluff is the cotton. It protects the plant's seeds, which are tucked inside it. The cotton is separated from the seeds, washed, and pulled into long fibers. The fibers are then spun into cotton yarns. This is done by taking several fibers and twisting them together to form one long strand.

Cotton yarns are woven over and under each other to make cloth. When the cloth eventually wears out, some of the fibers become loose and break.

COTTON BELT

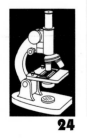

- In Tehucan Valley, Mexico, cotton remnants have been discovered that are seven thousand years old.
- The United States is one of the world's biggest cotton producers. The Cotton Belt stretches from Florida to North Carolina as far west as California.

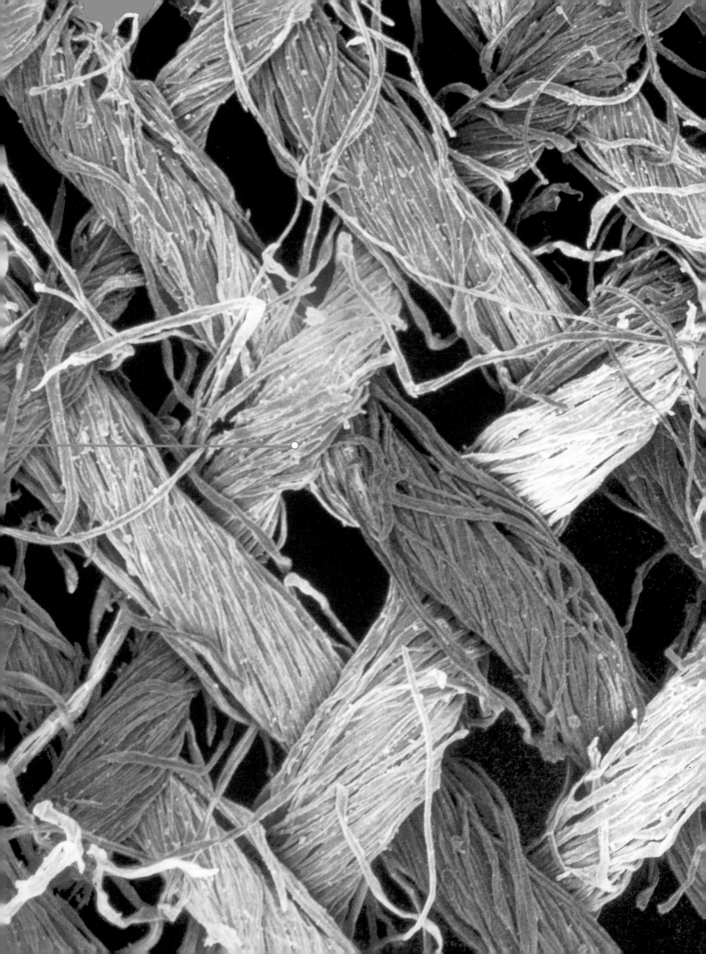

HOUSE HAUNTERS

Cockroaches are common house-hold pests that spread disease. Cockroaches are found in houses and other buildings — especially old structures — where they live on human food and debris. Cockroaches are hard to control because they can run fast and disappear quickly into narrow cracks. The red-brown American cockroach can reach up to 1.5 inches (3.8 cm) in length. Like other cockroaches, the red-brown American type can fly and is an excellent climber.

Like all insects, the cockroach has three pairs of legs. A cockroach is able to grip smooth surfaces with a footpad and double claw at the end of each foot.

ANCIENT INSECTS

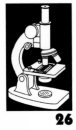

- Cockroaches are among the oldest insects on Earth. Their fossils are found in many places in North America, Europe, and the northern parts of Asia. Some of them date back to the Carboniferous Period of Earth's history which occurred between 345 million and 280 million years ago.

MODERN MIRACLE

A Band-Aid may look simple and uncomplicated, but it is the result of a great deal of research. The pad of the Band-Aid covers the wound, protecting the wound from further injury. The pad also absorbs blood and pus. A special coating on the pad stops it from sticking to the wound. The plastic surrounding the pad is designed to allow the wound and the skin bordering the wound to breathe. A Band-Aid is coated with adhesive on one side, which keeps the pad in place. When the Band-Aid is removed, however, the adhesive does not stick to the skin.

Tiny pores, or openings, in the surface of a Band-Aid allow air to get to the wound. Cuts and other wounds heal more quickly when air reaches them.

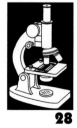

BAND-AID FIRST-AID

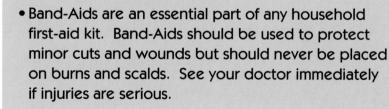

• Band-Aids are an essential part of any household first-aid kit. Band-Aids should be used to protect minor cuts and wounds but should never be placed on burns and scalds. See your doctor immediately if injuries are serious.

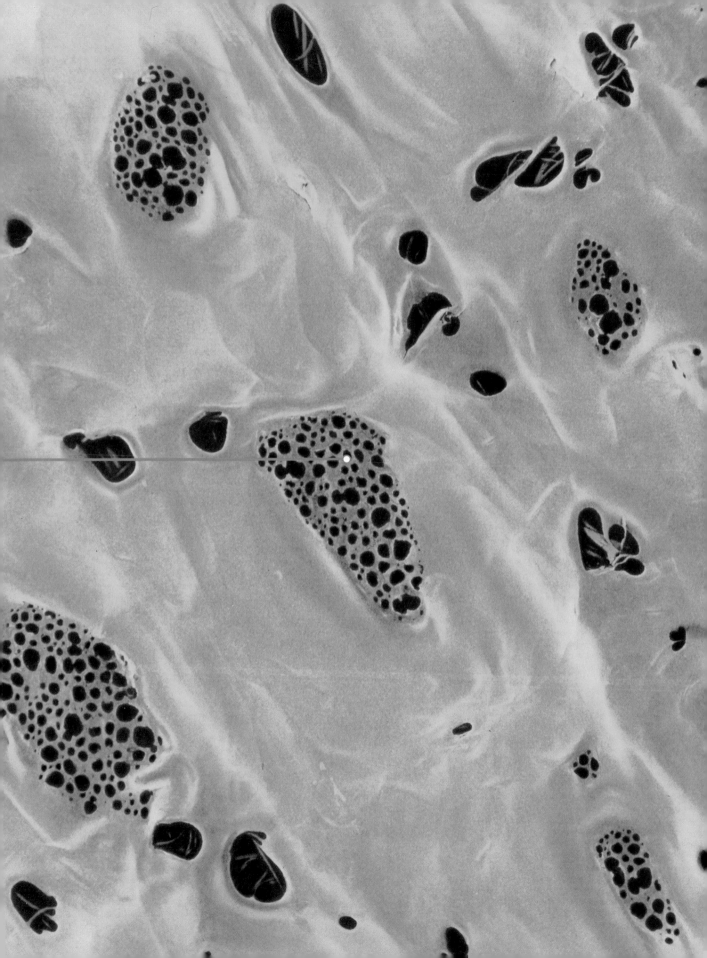

GLOSSARY

adhesive: a material or substance that secures objects together. Glue is an adhesive.

allergy: a strong, negative reaction to certain substances, especially dust, pollen, and foods. An allergy may result in breathing problems or a rash on the skin.

bacteria: tiny living organisms that are so small they can be seen only with a microscope. Many types of bacteria cause illnesses.

circuit: a circular system around which electricity flows.

fiber: a thin strand of material such as cotton, wool, or glass.

laser: a device that makes a special kind of concentrated light.

plastic: a synthetic, or human-made, material with many uses. When plastic is heated, it softens and can be shaped into various forms. Plastic hardens when it cools.

pollen: small, usually yellow grains that are the male part of a flower.

polyester: a human-made fiber that is made from liquid plastic.

polyurethane: a human-made substance that is used in the manufacture of flexible and rigid foams.

spinneret: a machine through which certain liquids are passed in order to make filaments.

transistor: a device that strengthens the electric current in electronic equipment.

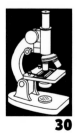

FURTHER STUDY

BOOKS

All About Allergies. Susan Terkel (Dutton)

Around the Home. Lionel Bender (Franklin Watts)

Cockroaches. Mona Kerby (Franklin Watts)

Determined to Win: Children Living with Allergies and Asthma. Thomas Bergman (Gareth Stevens)

Microaliens: Dazzling Journeys With an Electron Microscope. Howard Tomb (Farrar, Straus, & Giroux)

Plastics. Terry Cash (Garrett Educational Corp.)

Small Inventions That Make a Big Difference. Donald J. Crump (National Geographic Society)

VIDEOS

Homes. All Year Round series. (Journal Film and Video)

Ideas and Inventions. Full Option Science Systems series. (Encyclopædia Britannica)

The Microscope and Its Incredible World. (Barr Films)

Plastic Fantastic. (New Dimension Media)

Plastics. (Barr Films)

Videocassette. How It's Made series. (Lucerne Media)

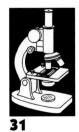

INDEX